Published by Barbour Publishing, Inc., P.O. Box 719, Uhrichsville, Ohio 44683
http://www.barbourbooks.com

Member of the
Evangelical Christian
Publishers Association

Printed in the United States of America.

My Country 'Tis of Thee

REBECCA GERMANY

BARBOUR
PUBLISHING, INC.
Uhrichsville, Ohio

America

My country, 'tis of thee,
Sweet land of liberty,
Of thee I sing.
Land where my fathers died!
Land of the Pilgrim's pride!
From ev'ry mountain side,
Let freedom ring.

My native country thee,
Land of the noble free,
Thy name I love;
I love thy rocks and rills,
Thy woods and templed hills;
My heart with rapture thrills
Like that above.

Let music swell the breeze,
And ring from all the trees
Sweet freedom's song.
Let mortal tongues awake;
Let all that breathe partake;
Let rocks their silence break,
The sound prolong.

Our father's God, to Thee,
Author of liberty,
To Thee we sing;
Long may our land be bright
With freedom's holy light;
Protect us by Thy might,
Great God, our King!

REV. SAMUEL FRANCIS SMITH
FEBRUARY 1832

My country, 'tis of thee,
sweet land of liberty,
of thee I sing.

O Lord our Heavenly Father, high and mighty King of kings, and Lord of lords, who dost from thy throne behold all the dwellers on earth and reignest with power supreme and uncontrolled over all the Kingdoms, Empires, and Governments; look down in mercy, we beseech thee, on these our American States, who have fled to thee from the rod of the oppressor and thrown themselves on Thy gracious protection, desiring to be henceforth dependent only on Thee. . . . Give them wisdom in Council and valor in the field; defeat the malicious designs of our cruel adversaries; . . .constrain them to drop the weapons of war from their unnerved bands in the day of battle!

Be Thou present, O God of wisdom, and direct the councils of this honorable assembly; enable them to settle things on the best and surest foundation. That the scene of blood may be speedily closed; that order, harmony, and peace may be effectually restored, and truth and justice, religion, and piety, prevail and flourish amongst the people. . . . All this we ask in the name and through the merits of Jesus Christ, Thy Son and our Savior. Amen.

THE FIRST PRAYER OFFERED IN CONGRESS
SEPTEMBER 7, 1774 BY JACOB DUCHE

"*We* have been assured, Sir, in the sacred writings, that 'except the Lord building the House they labour in vain that build it.' . . .I therefore beg leave to move that henceforth prayers imploring the assistance of heaven, and its blessings on our deliberations be held in this Assembly every morning before we proceed to business. . . ."

BEN FRANKLIN
PHILADELPHIA CONSTITUTIONAL CONVENTION, 1787

"*It* cannot be emphasized too strongly or too often that this great nation was founded not by religionists but by Christians, not on religion but on the gospel of Jesus Christ. We shall not fight alone. God presides over the destinies of nations. The battle is not to the strong alone. Is life so dear, or peace so sweet, as to be purchased at the price of chains and slavery? Forbid it, ALMIGHTY GOD! Give me liberty or give me death!"

PATRICK HENRY
PHILADELPHIA CONSTITUTIONAL CONVENTION, 1787

"*The* highest story of the American Revolution is this: it connected in one indissoluble bond the principles of civil government with the principles of Christianity."

PRESIDENT JOHN ADAMS

"*Every* thinking man, when he thinks, realizes that the teachings of the Bible are so interwoven and entwined with our whole civic and social life that it would be literally—I do not mean figuratively, but literally—impossible for us to figure what that loss would be if these teachings were removed. We would lose all the standards by which we now judge both public and private morals; all the standards towards which we, with more or less resolution, strive to raise ourselves."

PRESIDENT THEODORE ROOSEVELT

"*The* fundamental basis of this nation's law was given to Moses on the Mount. The fundamental basis of our Bill of Rights comes from the teaching we get from Exodus and St. Matthew, from Isaiah and St. Paul. I don't think we emphasize that enough these days."

PRESIDENT HARRY S. TRUMAN

Land where my fathers died

"It is rather for us to be here dedicated to the great task remaining before us—that from these honored dead we take increased devotion to that cause for which they gave the last full measure of devotion—that we here highly resolve that these dead shall not have died in vain, that this nation under God shall have a new birth of freedom, and that government of the people, by the people, for the people shall not perish from the earth."

PRESIDENT ABRAHAM LINCOLN

GETTYSBURG ADDRESS

"As we have been assured, neither death nor life, nor angels nor principalities nor powers, nor things present nor things to come, nor height nor depth, can separate us from God's love. May He bless the souls of the departed. May He comfort our own. And may He always guide our country. God bless America."

PRESIDENT GEORGE W. BUSH

SEPTEMBER 14, 2001 FROM THE NATIONAL CATHEDRAL

Land of the Pilgrim's pride

"*It* is hoped that by God's assistance, some of the continents in the ocean will be discovered. . .for the glory of God."

CHRISTOPHER COLUMBUS

"*Go ye into all the world, and preach the gospel to every creature.*"

MARK 16:15

"*James,* by the grace of god, king of England, Scotland, France, and Ireland, defender of the faith, . . . Whereas, upon the humble petition. . .of our well disposed subjects, that intended to make several plantations in the parts of America. . .in hope thereby to advance the enlargement of Christian religion, to the glory of God Almighty. . . ."

KING JAMES I
THE NEW ENGLAND CHARTER OF 1620

"In the name of God, amen. We, whose names are underwritten, the loyal subjects of our dread sovereign lord, King James, by the grace of God, of England, France and Ireland, king, defender of the Faith, etc. Having undertaken for the glory of God, and advancement of the Christian faith, and the honor of our king and country, a voyage to plant the first colony in the northern parts of Virginia. . ."

FORTY-ONE LEADERS OF THE PILGRIMS
MAYFLOWER COMPACT
NOVEMBER 11, 1620

"Being thus arrived in a good harbor and brought safe to land, they fell upon their knees and blessed the God of heaven."

GOVERNOR WILLIAM BRADFORD
OF PLYMOUTH PLANTATION

"Lastly and chiefly the way to prosper and achieve good success is to make yourselves all of one mind for the good of your country and your own, and to serve and fear God the giver of all goodness, for every plantation which our heavenly Father hath not planted shall be rooted out."

INSTRUCTIONS FOR THE VIRGINIA COLONY 1606

From every mountain side,
let freedom ring.

"Proclaim liberty
throughout all the land
unto all the inhabitants thereof."

LEVITICUS 25:10
INSCRIPTION ON THE LIBERTY BELL

"The Almighty God has blessed our land in many ways. He has given our people stout hearts and strong arms with which to strike mighty blows for freedom and truth. He has given to our country a faith which has become the hope of all peoples in an anguished world."

FRANKLIN D. ROOSEVELT
FOURTH PRESIDENTIAL INAUGURAL ADDRESS
SATURDAY, JANUARY 20, 1945

My native country thee,
Land of the noble free,
Thy name I love;
I love thy rocks and rills,
Thy woods and templed hills;
My heart with rapture thrills
Like that above.

Home, Sweet Home

Mid pleasures and palaces though we may roam,
Be it ever so humble, there's no place like home;
A charm from the skies seems to hallow us there,
Which, seek thro' the world, is ne'er met with elsewhere.
Home, home, sweet, sweet home.

JOHN HOWARD PAYNE (1792–1852)
AMERICAN FOLK SONG

"My God! How little do my countrymen
know what precious blessings they are in possession of,
and which no other people on earth enjoy!"

PRESIDENT THOMAS JEFFERSON

Let music swell the breeze,
And ring from all the trees
Sweet freedom's song.
Let mortal tongues awake;
Let all that breathe partake;
Let rocks their silence break,
The sound prolong.

America, the Beautiful

O beautiful for spacious skies,
For amber waves of grain,
For purple mountain majesties
Above the fruited plain!

America! America! God shed His grace on thee,
And crown thy good with brotherhood,
From sea to shining sea.

O beautiful for patriot dream
That sees beyond the years
Thine alabaster cities gleam,
Undimmed by human tears!

America! America! God shed His grace on thee,
And crown thy good with brotherhood,
From sea to shining sea.

KATHERINE LEE BATES, 1893

Our father's God! To Thee,
Author of liberty,
to Thee we sing.

"*We* hold these truths to be self-evident, that all men are created equal, that they are endowed by their Creator with certain unalienable rights, that among these are Life, Liberty, and the pursuit of Happiness."

THOMAS JEFFERSON
THE DECLARATION OF INDEPENDENCE

"*Human* law must rest its authority ultimately upon the authority of that law which is divine. . . . Far from being rivals or enemies, religion and law are twin sisters, friends and mutual assistants. Indeed, these two sciences run into each other."

JAMES WILSON,
A SIGNER OF THE CONSTITUTION
AND AN ORIGINAL JUSTICE ON THE U.S. SUPREME COURT

"The reason that Christianity is the best friend of government is because Christianity is the only religion that changes the heart."

PRESIDENT THOMAS JEFFERSON

"The religion which has introduced civil liberty is the religion of Christ and His Apostles. . . . This is genuine Christianity, and to this we owe our free constitutions of government."

NOAH WEBSTER (1758–1843)
AMERICAN LEXICOGRAPHER

*"If we make religion our business,
God will make it our blessedness."*

PRESIDENT JOHN ADAMS

"And to the same Divine Author of every good and perfect gift [James 1:17] we are indebted for all those privileges and advantages, religious as well as civil, which are so richly enjoyed in this favored land."

PRESIDENT JAMES MADISON

*"The Bible is the Rock
on which this Republic rests."*

PRESIDENT ANDREW JACKSON

"*In* no other place in the United States are there so many, and such varied official evidences of deep and abiding faith in God on the part of governments as there are in Washington. . . . Inasmuch as our great leaders have shown no doubt about God's proper place in the American birthright, can we, in our day, dare do less?"

SENATOR ROBERT BIRD, 196

"*The heritage of the past is the seed that brings forth the harvest of the future.*"

INSCRIBED ON THE STATUE "HERITAGE"
FLANKING THE NATIONAL ARCHIVES BUILDING, WASHINGTON, D.C.

God of Our Fathers

God of our fathers, whose almighty hand
Leads forth in beauty all the starry band
Of shining worlds in splendor through the skies,
Our grateful songs before Thy throne arise.

Thy Love divine hath led us in the past,
In this free land by Thee our lot is cast;
Be Thou our ruler, guardian, guide, and stay,
Thy word our law, Thy paths our chosen way.

From war's alarms, from deadly pestilence,
Be Thy strong arm our ever sure defense;
Thy true religion in our hearts increase,
Thy bounteous goodness nourish us in peace.

Refresh Thy people on their toilsome way,
Lead us from night to never ending day;
Fill our lives with love and grace divine,
And glory, laud, and praise be ever Thine!

DANIEL C. ROBERTS

Long may our land be bright
with freedom's holy light.

"*Religion, morality, and knowledge are necessary to good government, the preservation of liberty, and the happiness of mankind.*"

UNITED STATES SUPREME COURT, 1892

Oh! thus be it ever, when freemen shall stand
Between their loved homes and the war's desolation!
Blest with victory and peace, may the heaven-rescued land
Praise the Power that hath made and preserved us a nation!
Then conquer we must, for our cause it is just,
And this be our motto: "In God is our trust!"
And the star-spangled banner in triumph shall wave
O'er the land of the free and the home of the brave!

FRANCES SCOTT KEY (1779–1843)
RARELY SEEN LAST VERSE
OF "THE STAR SPANGLED BANNER"

"Ye are the light of the world.
A city that is set on a hill cannot be hid."

MATTHEW 5:14

May God save the Union! Still, still may it stand
upheld by the strength of the patriot hand,
to cement it our Fathers ensanguined the sod,
to keep it we kneel to a merciful God.

FROM A PATRIOTIC HYM

"*Heavenly* Father, we bow our heads and thank You for Your love. Accept our thanks for the peace that yields this day and the shared faith that makes its continuance likely. Make us strong to do Your work, willing to heed and hear Your will, and write on our hearts these words: 'Use power to help people.' For we are given power not to advance our own purposes, nor to make a great show in the world, nor a name. There is but one just use of power, and it is to serve people. Help us to remember it, Lord. Amen."

GEORGE BUSH
PRESIDENTIAL INAUGURAL ADDRESS
FRIDAY, JANUARY 20, 1989

Protect us by thy might,
great God, our King!

"I will lift up mine eyes unto the hills,
from whence cometh my help.
My help cometh from the LORD,
which made heaven and earth."

PSALM 121:1–2

"Whereas it is the duty of all Nations to acknowledge the providence of Almighty God, to obey His will, to be grateful for His benefits, and humbly to implore His protection and favor, and whereas both Houses of Congress have by their joint committee requested me to recommend to the People of the United States a day of public thanks-giving and prayer to be observed by acknowledging with grateful hearts the many single favors of Almighty God, especially by affording them an opportunity peaceably to establish a form of government for their safety and happiness."

PRESIDENT GEORGE WASHINGTON
THANKSGIVING DAY PROCLAMATION

How Firm a Foundation

Fear not, I am with thee; O be not dismayed,
For I am thy God, and will still give thee aid;
I'll strengthen thee, help thee, and cause thee to stand,
Upheld by My righteous, omnipotent hand.

TRADITIONAL HYM

"*O Lord,* when we, Thy children, are apprehensive about the affairs of our world, remind us that Thou art in Thy world as well as above and beyond it. Remind us that Thou art not indifferent. For Thou art not a spectator God, high and lifted up, serene and unperturbed. The feet that were wounded are still walking the trails of earth. The heart that was broken on the tree still feels every human woe."

PETER MARSHALL
CHAPLAIN, U.S. SENATE, 1947–1949

O God, Our Help in Ages Past

O God, our help in ages past, Our hope for years to come,
Our shelter from the stormy blast, And our eternal home!

Before the hills in order stood, Or earth received her frame,
From everlasting thou art God, To endless years the same.

A thousand ages, in thy sight, Are like an evening gone;
Short as the watch that ends the night, Before the rising sun.

Time, like an ever-rolling stream, Bears all its sons away;
They fly forgotten, as a dream Dies at the opening day.

O God, our help in ages past, Our hope for years to come,
Be thou our guide while life shall last, And our eternal home!

ISAAC WATTS (1674–174

BASED ON PSALM

"*If* we fail now, we shall have forgotten in abundance what we learned in hardship: that democracy rests on faith, that freedom asks more than it gives, and that the judgment of God is harshest on those who are most favored."

LYNDON BAINES JOHNSON
PRESIDENTIAL INAUGURAL ADDRESS
WEDNESDAY, JANUARY 20, 1965

"Blessed is the nation whose God is the LORD."

PSALM 33:12

"If my people, which are called by my name,
shall humble themselves, and pray, and seek my face,
and turn from their wicked ways; then will I hear from heaven,
and will forgive their sin, and will heal their land."

2 CHRONICLES 7:14

"*We* have been the recipients of the choicest bounties of heaven. We have been preserved, these many years, in peace and prosperity. We have grown in numbers, wealth, and power, as no other nation has ever grown. But we have forgotten God. We have forgotten the gracious hand which preserved us in peace, and multiplied and enriched and strengthened us; and we have vainly imagined, in the deceitfulness of our hearts, that all these blessings were produced by some superior wisdom and virtue of our own. Intoxicated with unbroken success, we have become too self-sufficient to feel the necessity of redeeming and pre-serving grace, too proud to pray to the God that made us! It behooves us, then to humble ourselves before the offended Power, to confess our national sins, and to pray for clemency and forgiveness."

PRESIDENT ABRAHAM LINCOLN
APRIL 30, 1863, PROCLAMATION FOR A NATIONAL DAY
OF FASTING, HUMILIATION, AND PRAYER

"*The* choice before us is plain, Christ or chaos, conviction or compromise, discipline or disintegration. I am rather tired of hearing about our rights and privileges as American citizens. The time is come, it now is, when we ought to hear about the duties and responsibilities of our citizenship. America's future depends upon demonstrating God's government."

PETER MARSHALL
CHAPLAIN, U.S. SENATE, 1947–19